MAU
HAN
HIGHWAY

A VISITOR'S GUIDE

Beautiful storm surf, Ke'anae Peninsula.

by Angela Kay Kepler

Mutual Publishing

1

East Wailuaiki Stream (near Nahiku) is one of the hundreds of waterfalls that tumble off Haleakala's well-watered slopes.

Printed in Japan.

Copyright 1995 by: Mutual Publishing
                       1127 11th Avenue, Mezz. B
                       Honolulu, Hawaii 96816
                       Tel (808) 732-1709 / Fax (808) 734-4094

Library of Congress Catalog Card No. 87-061315

TABLE OF CONTENTS

BALDWIN PARK, close to Pa'ia, provides gorgeous views of the West Maui Mountains from its extensive coconut palm-lined beach, complete with picnic ground, camping area, and some children's facilities.

ACKNOWLEDGEMENTS

Symbolic of tropical beauty, bougainvillea (*Bougainvillea* species) is a common garden plant everywhere on Maui.

I would like to express my thanks to the many friends and relatives who hiked or drove with me on, above or below the Hana Highway. Their different eyes and perspectives expanded my vision and refreshed my enthusiasm for Maui's beauty. Special gratitude is extended to members of the Mauna Ala Hiking Club, the Sierra Club, and the U.S. Fish & Wildlife Service. Bob Hobdy and Mary Evanson, especially, were always eager for new adventures.

To obtain the photos from unusual viewpoints, there were many who shared tents, pouring rain, biting winds, pesty mosquitoes, scorching sun, squashed sandwiches, dwindling water supplies and precious morsels of chocolate. Tom Hauptman plucked me from many remote locations in his helicopter, often under perilous flying conditions.

Thanks are also due to those who augmented my color transparencies (see photo credits); to Ron Lester for drafting the map, and Hugo Huntzinger and the Hawaii Natural History Association for proofreading.

Lastly, I wish to acknowledge the early training from my parents and teachers, and the good behavior of our children, Sylvelin and Leilani. My husband Cameron helped provide opportunities for field work, proofread the manuscript, assisted with photography and contributed companionship and stimulation both in the field and home.

To all, my heartfelt thanks.

PREFACE

In a similar manner to the way in which concert program notes enhance one's appreciation of music, this book is intended to enrich one's experience of the noted drive to Hana.

It is essentially a picture book, divided into 14 sections each corresponding to a variable length of road (see map).

Hopefully it will answer questions relating to plants, birds, mammals, geology, weather, Hawaiian culture and conservation of natural resources. You can safely munch on sweet guavas without worrying about food poisoning, identify sights and flowers along the way, and most importantly, enjoy the drive even if you never reach Hana.

This twisting, narrow, mountain highway is an end in itself. It is not a road to be whizzed around in haste to reach a certain destination, such as driving from Los Angeles to San Diego for a business meeting. Stop frequently and let its expansive views, colors, smells and sounds seep into you. They all contribute to a collective ambience. If you rush, you will miss very personal island sentiments that would otherwise have remained with you long after your trip.

Relish the continual flow of audio-visual beauty along the Hana Highway, just as you would enjoy the progression of your favorite music as it weaves, moment by moment, through space.

DO'S AND DON'TS ON THE HANA HIGHWAY

DO'S

- Fill up with gasoline in Kahului or Pa'ia. There are no service stations until you reach Hana. • Take food and drink. Only snacks are available en route. • Take a raincoat (and plastic bags for cameras, etc.) if you plan on leaving your car even for a few minutes. • Watch children closely. The ground is generally muddy, the rocks are slippery and the steep cliffs are dangerous.

DON'TS

- Drink water from streams or water flows from pig-infested forests or cow pastures. You may easily get sick. • Dive into pools. • Swim in the ocean at Kipahulu. • Cross streams (e.g. en route to Waimoku Falls) if river is high. • Walk too far from the road unless along established trails. Most land is privately owned.
- Rush, especially from Hana to Kipahulu. The road is poor, narrow and winding.
- Let children play on rock walls. Most are ancient and/or have special significance to the Hawaiian people. • Drive rental cars beyond Kipahulu (jeeps are fine IF the road is open).

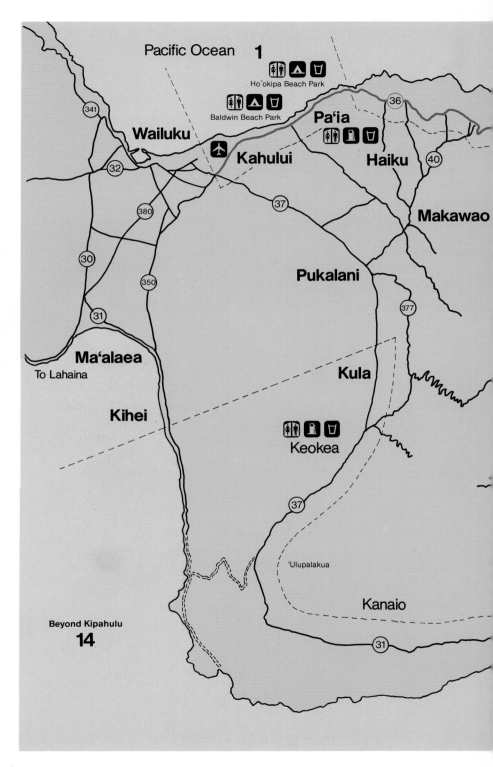

Pacific Ocean **1**

Ho'okipa Beach Park

Baldwin Beach Park

Wailuku

Pa'ia

Kahului

Haiku

Makawao

Pukalani

Ma'alaea

To Lahaina

Kula

Kihei

Keokea

'Ulupalakua

Kanaio

Beyond Kipahulu
14

341 36 40 32 380 37 30 350 31 377 37 31

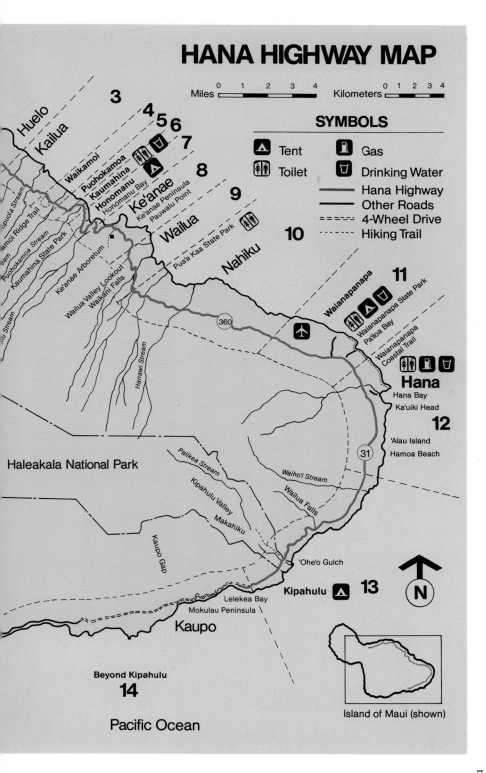

HANA HIGHWAY MAP

Miles 0 1 2 3 4   Kilometers 0 1 2 3 4

SYMBOLS

⛺	Tent	⛽	Gas
🚻	Toilet	🚰	Drinking Water

Hana Highway
Other Roads
4-Wheel Drive
Hiking Trail

Huelo
Kailua
3
4 5 6
7
Waikamoi
Puohokamoa
Kaumahina
Honomanu
Honomanu Bay
Ke'anae
Ke'anae Peninsula
Pauwalu Point
8
Wailua
9
Pua'a Kaa State Park
Nahiku
10
11
Waianapanapa
Waianapanapa State Park
Pailoa Bay
Waianapanapa
Coastal Trail

Hana
Hana Bay
Ka'uiki Head
12
'Alau Island
Hamoa Beach

'Ōpuola Stream
Kailua Stream
Waikamoi Ridge Trail
Puohokamoa Stream
Kaumahina State Park
Ke'anae Arboretum
Wailua Valley Lookout
Waikani Falls
Hanawi Stream

360
31

Haleakala National Park
Palikea Stream
Kipahulu Valley
Makahiku
Waiho'i Stream
Wailua Falls
Kaupo Gap
'Ohe'o Gulch

Kipahulu
13

Lelekea Bay
Mokulau Peninsula
Kaupo

Beyond Kipahulu
14

Pacific Ocean

N

Island of Maui (shown)

PA'IA

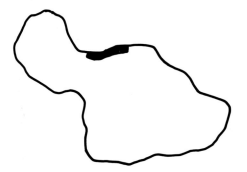

A few miles east of Kahului the Hana Highway (Route 36) skirts the airport amidst acres of sugar cane, then heads on through the partially revived old plantation town of *Pa'ia* (pron. "Pie-*ee*-ah"), the last commercial center before Hana. In addition to supplying items necessary for the long drive around Maui's north shore, this colorful spot is an art center for island-created handicrafts (Maui Crafts' Guild). Potential picnickers should check out a country store or a food-to-go shop.

Don't forget to fill your car up with gasoline; there's none available until you reach Hana — 52 miles, 617 curves and 56 bridges later.

Pa'ia is an excellent area from which to observe 10,000 foot Haleakala, the enormous dormant volcano that dominates East Maui and provides the spectacular topography ahead.

The best beaches along the entire highway are right here: Baldwin, and Ho'okipa, world-renowned for its superb waves, ideal for the exciting sports of surfing and wind-surfing. A local favorite, Ho'okipa is nevertheless dangerous to swimmers unaccustomed to high surf, strong currents and rocky coastlines. Covered pavilions overlooking the coast provide an excellent breakfast spot for early birds driving towards Hana.

A window of late afternoon light highlights
IAO VALLEY (West Maui Mts.) as seen from Pa'ia,
the beginning of Maui's famous Hana Highway.

The staff of life on other Pacific Islands, **COCONUT PALMS** (*Cocos nucifera*) are little-used in Hawaii. Look closely at the tall palms dotted around Baldwin Beach and you may spy a palm-trimmer (most likely a Tongan) hacking energetically at dead fronds and developing nuts. These men are always happy to share fresh coconut water with you. Coconuts are well insulated by thick stringy fibers, and draughts of their transparent liquid always taste refreshingly cool.

The Kahului-Pa'ia area is dominated by **SUGARCANE,** one of Maui's major industries. Covering almost 50,000 acres, Maui's sugar totals 300,000 tons each year.

HIBISCUS (*Hibiscus* species) bloom all year in Pa'ia, as elsewhere on Maui. Each bloom will last at least one day without water.

Freshly painted, the **PA'IA GENERAL STORE,** a revitalized outgrowth of the alternate lifestyle (hippie) movement of the 60's and 70's, is the last chance for food (except for a few roadside stands) until Hana.

PA'IA MANTOKUGI MISSION, with its shapely oriental architecture, colorful cemetery and authentic Japanese gong, is remindful of the strong Buddhist faith of many Maui residents.

During summer, the **ROYAL POINCIANA** *(Delonix regia)* bursts forth with a mass of orange flowers.

HO'OKIPA BEACH PARK.

Surfers and windsurfers skim down waves powered by arctic storms. Inshore wave intensity is broken by an inner sandstone ledge, enabling toddlers to play safely in shallow pools adjacent to the sandy area. Pool size depends on tides, surf height and amount of sand. For older children, a jacuzzi-like circular pool gauged in the ledge provides hours of enjoyment, as does a small swimming area at the east end. Fishermen favor rocky areas by the cliffs. While camping is free, with no permit required, it is windy.

Whether tortuously tossing amidst the fury of a storm, breaking with turquoise and glassy edges, or arching back in curving rooster tails, Ho'okipa's waves are ever-changing and ever-beautiful. Their shape, color, and dynamism add another dimension to Maui's natural beauty. Each of four major surfing breaks accommodates surfers of varying levels of competence.

You may be lucky to strike a **WINDSURFING** practice day, even a championship meet, when the water is flecked with brilliantly colored, dynamic "sea butterflies". Admire these skillful wave riders from the elevated parking areas above the cliffs.

Particularly familiar to lowlanders, the **GIANT NEO-TROPICAL TOAD** (known locally as "bufo" or "poloka") may be encountered sleeping in roadside grass, hunting in moist gardens during the day, or pitifully squashed on roads after dark. Chunky and squat, with warty, dry skin, these toads were brought to Hawaii from Puerto Rico in 1932 in efforts to control a plethora of alien insects plaguing sugar cane fields. Watch for their large tadpoles crowding muddy ponds along the highway or, if you are traveling at night, listen for their deep, throaty croaks penetrating the otherwise quiet air.

HAIKU

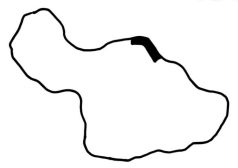

Pineapples! Their presence indicates a changing climate. Maui's semi-arid isthmus ("valley"), supporting expanses of irrigated sugar, is now left behind. Haiku, hidden close upslope, receives over fifty inches of rain annually in contrast to Pa'ia's thirty inches, and is cooler and more humid.

The Haiku (pron. "High-*ku*") area is fronted by cliffs of ever-increasing height as the sea nips into Haleakala. Concealed waterfalls plunge into lush precipitous valleys and waves crash mightily against rocky headlands.

Here is the last easy section of travel until Hana. Twisting gently, the real Hana Highway begins (renumbered 360) at the junction with Hwy. 40. Soon the writhing narrow mountain road will slow traffic to a crawl.

Now is the time for new sights, tastes, smells and sounds. The grip of civilization loosens. Don't worry if you run into a rain squall; it may (or may not) be clear ahead.

While driving this first section, notice gradual transformations as the road moves onto Haleakala's ever-steepening flank. Although pasturelands that have replaced pineapple fields persist, roadside grasses are progressively yielding to ferns and Philippine ground orchids, whose clusters of small mauve flowers beautify the roadcuts. In fine weather, note the dark green of native forests at higher elevations (especially visible at mile marker 13), while around you a patchy assemblage of introduced trees comprise Maui's windward lowland forests, notably ironwood, Norfolk Island pine, christmas berry, *kukui*, guava, mango and Java plum (the last three are edible).

Aerial view of **PINEAPPLE FIELDS** curving around Kuiaha Bay.

Seaward of the Hana Highway lies a **RUGGED COASTLINE** replete with steep valleys, lush vegetation, waterfalls, bays, islands, and rocky points, accessible for the most part, only to hardy hikers.

PASSIONFRUIT: visions of aphrodisiacs and their associated delights spring to mind as one contemplates this delectable tropical fruit. When first named by Spanish settlers in tropical America, passionfruits reminded them not of worldly pleasures but the sufferings of Christ. Each portion of their curious flowers symbolized one aspect of the crucifixion: the ten petals represented the apostles, the "fringed crown" the crown of thorns, the three knobbed styles the holy trinity, etc. Shining brilliantly green in backlighted growth, the vine's lobed leaves, portraying the fingered hands of Christ's prosecutors, are a common sight in small gullies.

In India, Buddha is sometimes pictured sitting beneath the **ROSE APPLE**'s *(Eugenia jambos)* full-foliaged branches. Bearing abundant yellow pompom blossoms and pastel greenish-pink "fruits of immortality" from August to October, this tree was introduced from India as an ornamental. Most unusual is the delicate rose taste of its fruit. Its pinkish flesh is firm, tender, non-acidic, and sweet. Rose apples are best when fresh from the tree, very ripe or even bruised. Since escaping from cultivation, rose apple's dark thickets form characteristic components of our newly evolving lowland forests.

With fronds shaped like breadfruit leaves, the **LAUA'E** (pronounced "la-wah-ee") *Microsorium scolopendria*, is one of Maui's most attractive and well-known ferns. Its snaky green stems (rhizomes) creep and intertwine in mats along the ground, sending up shiny, upright, leathery leaves. Large, indented, circular spore clusters dot the frond's longer finger-like lobes on their undersides. In ancient Hawaii this fern symbolized romantic love.

Little purple clusters of **PHILIPPINE GROUND ORCHIDS** *(Spathoglottis plicata)*, peeking up through pleated leaves and roadside ferns, brighten the more open sections of the highway from Haiku to Kipahulu. Maui's own native orchids, now very rare, are restricted to drippy rainforests and high elevation bogs on Haleakala, more than a mile above.

14

Native to Brazil but common in Maui's lowlands, **CHRISTMAS-BERRY** *(Schinus terebinthifolius)* is most noticeable during the latter part of the year, when its dense clusters of scarlet berries brighten the roadside. Ideal for wreaths or decorations they are inedible, no matter how delectable they look.

Raucous, perky, and self-assured, **MYNAHS** are common in Hawaii's lowlands. These eight-inch brown birds, relatives of starlings, sport white wing patches that are conspicuous in flight. They were introduced from India in 1863 by Hawaii's sugar companies to combat caterpillars which nibbled on young cane shoots and threatened the existence of the sugar industry. Unfortunately the mynahs brought diseases that spread into the native bird populations, particularly Hawaii's unique honeycreepers, now restricted to higher elevations. Partial to fruits and berries, mynahs also disseminate weeds such as *Lantana,* a serious pasture pest. This mynah adorns a scarlet-flowering **TIGER'S CLAW** or **CORAL TREE** *(Erythrina variegata).*

Hop out of your car and you're bound to step on some tiny puffs of delicate pink, often in low, prickly mats. Touch a few leaves and they'll suddenly close up as though dead (little bladders at the base of the leaves release stored water that seeps into air spaces). A few minutes later, slowly at first, the entire **SENSITIVE PLANT** *(Mimosa pudica)* "comes alive" again. What a remarkable adaptation to avoid being eaten by mammals!

KAILUA

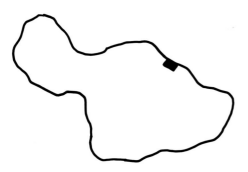

Neatly-trimmed gardens with colorful flowers greet you as you drive into this attractive outpost of civilization, field headquarters for the East Maui Irrigation Company (EMI). A company town, most residents work on the extensive ditch system that delivers water collected from Haleakala's north slope to central and up-country Maui (the State of Hawaii is unusual in that it allows private companies to share control of its water resources). Stop and look at the dams (particularly at mile marker 8), diversions, metal grids to keep out debris, and deep dark tunnels hand-hewn from the mountain.

Kailua (pron. "Kye-*loo*-ah") is a quiet town without even a store. What a dramatic change from the early 1900's, when criminals were banished to Kailua's prison camp, then the end of the road, from whence only a trail extended further east.

O'OPUOLA GULCH, one of dozens along the highway, affords a distant ocean view. Rounded masses of pale green, maple-like leaves of the *kukui (Aleurites moluccana)* tree typify such gullies, reminding us of olden times when people gathered the *kukui's* prolific oily nuts to create medicines, ingenious candles, and torches. Resembling tough-shelled walnuts, these fruits can cause intestinal distress if eaten. Their most recent use is to make shiny black seed leis sold in gift shops.

Over 50 miles of tunnels and 23 miles of ditches, mostly hand-hewn like these at O'opuola Gulch, comprise East Maui Irrigation's (EMI) **"DITCH SYSTEM,"** a monument to early 20th century Asian labor. If you plan to walk more than a stone's throw from your car (except at public stopping areas), or hunt pigs anywhere from Huelo to Waianapanapa, previous signed permission is necessary from the EMI office in Pa'ia. A State hunting license is also required.

Shady *kukui* and other roadside vegetation near Oopuola Gulch.

GUAVA TREES *(Psidium guajava)* are the most conspicuous shrub-bery along the highway until the wet, lush lowland forests. Lining roadsides and heavily dotting pastures, their rounded bushes, bearing circular, lemon-sized fruit, are unmistakable (top right). Select large, softish ones with rounded knobby skins and dark-pink flesh. Although acidic and seedy, guavas are sweet and tasty (bottom), and blend into delicious homemade juice. Pick all you desire, as this is a "weed" plant, but do respect "no trespassing" signs. And, as you note the fruitflies hovering around rotting, fallen fruit, don't even *think* of smuggling guavas back to the mainland!

Unfurling yellow in the morning, turning orange in the afternoon, and withering by nightfall, **HAU** (rhymes with cow), *Hibiscus tiliaceus* continually buds off heart-shaped leaves and hibiscus-shaped blossoms that signified the ephemeral human spirit to ancient Polynesians. Along certain sections of the highway (e.g., just past Kailua), roadworkers periodically expose impenetrable tangles of its lightweight branches. It's easy to understand why *hau* horrifies backpackers! An extremely useful coastal tree, *hau* provided an abundance of commodities for early Polynesian settlers, including cork-like fishing floats, medicines, ropes, clothing, and even a fire-making device.

Fragrant **YELLOW,** (right), **WHITE** (above) and **KAHILI** (below) **GINGERS** (*Hedychium* species), used for decoration and leis, are numerous along the entire Hana highway. Of Asian origin, their clusters of showy, butterfly-shaped flowers possess an irresistible odor. Even their pink rhizomes (which unfortunately choke out native vegetation) smell wonderful. Pick a blossom, nip off the bottom one-eighth inch and suck a few drops of its sweet, gingery nectar from the elongated flower tube. It's delicious.

18

ALLAMANDA'S (*Allamanda cathartica*) large, bright yellow, velvety flowers are unmistakable. A good area to spot their sprawling vines (which may climb trees) is just east of Kailua. From tropical Brazil, their three-inch tubular blossoms possess five rounded petals which expand from a deep brown throat.

Showy sprays of the **MOUNTAIN APPLE'S** (*Eugenia malaccensis*) cerise colored, miniature shaving brushes present a dazzling sight during May and June. Four or five months later, pink-and-white, waxy, thin-skinned fruits hang from their branches and trunks. Many trees seem to grow alongside steep gullies, their tempting fruits dangling just beyond reach. Juicy and pear-like, these "apples" were sacred to the Hawaiians of old, and are perfectly edible and tasty.

Don't be reticent about sampling the wild red or red-purple **STRAWBERRY GUAVAS** (*Psidium cattleianum*)! About one inch in diameter, and particularly prevalent in late summer and fall, these tasty fruits from Brazil make excellent jam as well as sweet, juicy snacks. Their shrubby trees, covered with glossy, elliptical leaves are, in places, replacing Maui's native forests.

19

WAIKAMOI

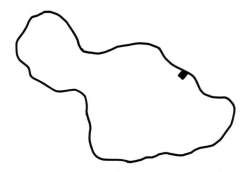

Winding through moist lowland forests the road almost leaves behind open country (see cover photo). Vegetation is wilder, more varied and, typical of all Hawaii's lowlands, introduced from other parts of the world: Asia, Australia, South America, and Polynesia.

The Waikamoi (meaning "water acquired by the threadfin fish" pron. "Why-ka-moy") region includes large stand of bamboo, eucalyptus, paperbark, gingers, heliconias and tropical vines.

Hawaii has no true "jungles" in the popular sense, nor is it a "tropical paradise," but from here to Kipahulu is the closest approximation on Maui to these overused phrases. As you pass through the bamboo forest, recall the wise words of Buddha, who loved to sit in bamboo groves, gently advising us that true paradise is "within."

One half-mile beyond mile marker 9 lies Waikamoi Ridge, where Hawaii's State Department of Land and Natural Resources (DLNR) has constructed a trail (no restrooms or water). Hop out of your car, stretch your legs and explore for five minutes or an hour. Smell the dank, earthy air, stroll through tall trees adorned with large, heart-shaped taro vines, peer closely at heliconia and ginger flowers, and admire the filtered light falling on lacy ferns. Maui has few public trails and this one is by far the most accessible, enabling one to experience the lush tropical forest.

HELICONIAS are popular ornamentals that lend a distinctive South American flavor to this portion of the Hana Highway (Hana is Hawaii's "heliconia capital"). The brilliant orange-red **LOBSTER CLAW** (*Heliconia bihai*), with banana-like leaves up to eight feet tall, derives its common name from a series of alternating "floral boats" the color of boiled lobsters. Within each claw-shaped and gracefully upcurved "boat" (actually a modified leaf) arise the true flowers—several inconspicuous, greenish blossoms. Due to the heavy rainfall in this area, the "boats" generally contain mushy water which creates ideal nurseries for mosquito and other insect larvae.

You may be lucky enough to spot a **"STAR FUNGUS"** (next to a fallen guava). Tropical and subtropical regions the world over are notoriously poor in mushrooms compared to colder regions, so it is always a pleasure to discover a gem such as this.

(Opposite page) Waikamoi is famous for its extensive **BAMBOO FOREST** (*Bambusa vulgaris*) which dates back into the realms of Hawaiian mythology. Generating an Oriental ambience, bamboo's jade-green or golden columns, sparsely mantled with feathery foliage, tower skywards. Locals collect its long conical shoots in summer (permits are necessary from DLNR) for incorporation into eastern dishes (unless properly cut, soaked, and pre-boiled they taste bitter). Creative Mauians also utilize bamboo's satin-smooth culms for Japanese-style flutes, elegant ornaments, and fishing poles.

21

Spirally festooning paper-bark and eucalyptus trees along **WAIKAMOI RIDGE TRAIL,** and lending a tropical flavor to the vegetation, these South American **TARO VINES** *(Scindapsus aureus)* are merely run-away houseplants!

Squeeze one of the reddish conical flowers of **SHAMPOO GINGER** *(Zingiber zerumbet),* the understory plant with wavy-edged leaves that lines Waikamoi Ridge Trail for quite a way. Enjoy its exotic fragrance. Introduced centuries ago into Hawaii, this three-foot high Polynesian, wild ginger exudes copious quantities of a perfumy, somewhat mucousy liquid that was used for a massage lubricant and shampoo before European man arrived.

Where the highway crosses Waikamoi Stream, a cliffside spring spills out in a trickling cascade that nurtures mosses and ferns, including delicate **MAIDENHAIR FERNS.** *(Adiantum raddianum).* A pipe taps this sweet, untainted water for all to enjoy (try some). Immediately above grows the uncommon, native **OLONA** *(Touchardia latifolia).* A non-stinging nettle, its large triangular leaves arise from flexible stems that yielded the strongest natural fibers in the world. Cordage from the thinnest threads to the thickest ship's hawsers were fabricated by Hawaiians using time-consuming methods involving soaking, beating, stripping and sun-bleaching.

PUOHOKAMOA

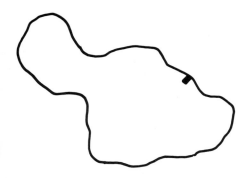

With waterfalls plunging into swimming-holes, deep abysses flanked by sheer cliffs, and rampant tropical vegetation, Puohokamoa typifies the rugged nature of Haleakala's north slope. At mile marker 11, where the highway crosses Puohokamoa Stream, a few cars can squeeze into a roadside pullout. From the bridge you can view a small, two-channeled waterfall: a short gravel trail leads to a pool at its base. A mini-picnic ground has been developed there, with a covered table in case you get caught by the rain (remember, rainforests are beautiful *because* of the rain they receive).

A brief walk along the path will quickly lead you through a sampling of lush vegetation typical of Maui's entire Hana Highway: *kukui* nut trees, *ti,* heliconias, impatiens, gingers, etc., all mingled with entwining vines.

An extremely short, sturdy trail tunnels through a rich profusion of tropical plants to a double waterfall and swimming hole at Puohokamoa Stream.

Yellow gingers and bunchy **TI** *(Cordyline terminalis)* leaves range wildly beneath the maple-like *kukui* trees. Prior to the days of foil, Saran Wrap, aspirins, beer, plates, flags, and raincoats, the Polynesian-introduced *ti*, with its big shiny, elliptical leaves served a variety of household, community, and "military" purposes.

Below the road (and invisible from it), Puohokamoa steepens into an incredibly dangerous **V-SHAPED VALLEY** (note car in photo). A ribbon waterfall plunges more than 200 feet into a shallow pool, from which ascent is practically impossible. Such terrain allows us to glimpse the numerous topographic difficulties faced by the highway's original construction workers, and is an impressive demonstration of the enduring victory of water over rock.

At Puohokamoa you are at 550 feet elevation, slightly more than a half mile from the sea. Offshore and inaccessible from land lies a picturesque, double-humped sea stack. **KEOPUKA ROCK,** 140 feet high, defies climbing, and is thus a haunt only for a few seabirds such as the graceful black noddies that scream around its cliffs searching for inshore fish. Coastal plants, some rare, cling precariously to its near-vertical sides.

For several miles you have passed road banks blanketed with Hawaii's native **FALSE STAGHORN FERN** (*uluhe, Dicranopteris linearis*). Its hardy fronds, about one foot across, divide successfully in twos, producing tangled mats of apple-green fernery which colonize and protect steep slopes from erosion. Higher on the banks Australian paperbark trees (related to eucalyptus) line the sky. *Uluhe* looks quite innocuous as you drive along, but try negotiating a ridge of it. Stiff entangling stems bind together tight greenery which can rise up to twenty feet high in compact thickets that challenge the staunchest hikers.

Maui's newest "Garden of Eden Arboretum," located on the Hana Highway just west of Puohokumoa Falls. One of its goals is to cultivate selected native Hawaiian and Polynesian introduced plants. Several miles of maintained trails wind amid lush lowland forests. Since the climate here is conducive to subtropical growth, trees and shrubs from other South Pacific islands and continental rainforests are also featured. Most plants are labelled with common and scientific names. In 1995, this garden received recognition from the State of Hawaii for its conservation theme and land management techniques.

THE MUDDY WATER STORY

Visitors and residents alike wonder why water flowing over the Hana Highway's waterfalls is so muddy, and whether it is safe to drink.

Rain forests above the highway, extending across the entire windward slope of Haleakala, contain large populations of introduced feral pigs, whose rooting and "rototilling" activities, coupled with steep slopes and heavy rainfall, cause extensive damage to Maui's watersheds. Native forests between 2500 and 7000 feet elevation are particularly vulnerable. The resultant erosion degrades Maui's water quality, destroys the pristine forests, introduces diseases, endangers birds and plants, produces the muddy water which flows over waterfalls, and creates mucky swimming in otherwise delightful swimming holes. Maui's streams contain bacterial counts which exceed federal standards: DO NOT DRINK STREAM WATER.

Native Hawaiian rain forests. Left: **PRISTINE VEGETATION,** fast diminishing on Maui. Right: **PIG-DAMAGED VEGETATION,** now more the rule than the exception.

A **PILE OF FOREST DEBRIS,** the result of a single storm and previously pig-damaged soil cover, measured 300 feet long, and averaged twelve feet wide and three feet high on a beach below the Hana Highway. This impressive mass of leaf litter was washed down by a single stream.

(Top right) Cute to play with when *keiki* (young ones) and exciting to hunt when mature, **WILD PIGS** were not originally part of Hawaii's native fauna.

KAUMAHINA

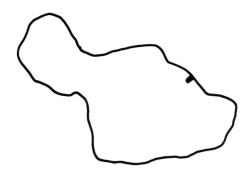

Stop at Kaumahina (literally "moonrise," pron. "Cow-mah-*hee*-nah") for a dramatic coastal view that provides your first glimpse of the picturesque, deeply-carved Honomanu Bay. Further east the

relatively fresh lavas of Ke'anae Peninsula, and an assortment of odd-shaped sea-stacks and rocky points, skirted with white foam, jut into rough waters.

Only 1.2 miles beyond Puohokamoa, this is the first stop since Pa'ia for tap drinking water, flush toilets, refuse bins and spacious picnic facilities (two tables are covered). Although it is approximately half-way to Hana, much of the best scenery lies ahead.

As you stretch your legs, note some of the beautiful tropical plants that thrive here on Maui's warm, wet north slope: red, shell, and torch gingers; spider lilies and giant white birds-of-paradise, all under a tree cover of paperbarks, eucalyptus and the golden-flowered Formosan koa. A nature trail also offers pleasant sauntering amongst tall *hala* trees, perched on tepee-like stilt roots.

SPECTACULAR COASTAL VIEW from Kaumahina State Wayside Park. Note Ke'anae peninsula jutting into the ocean, formed from lava flowing seaward from Haleakala.

Composed of numerous layers of pink-red waxy frills, the conical or tooth-shaped flowerheads of **TORCH GINGER** *(Etlingera elatior)* bespeak the luxuriant tropics Again Nature fools us — the petal-like frills overlapping in pinecone fashion, are not petals at all but fancy leaves! The true flowers (small, red and yellow) peek out from between the frilly layers. Look for these tall, magnificent blooms, dwarfed by their own leaves (up to twenty feet high), behind the bathrooms.

WEDELIA's *(Wedelia trilobata)* dandelion-like daisies, originally from South America, flourish anywhere, sending out creeping runners covered with bright green leaves. You've seen this cheery ground cover in gardens, parks, around hotels and banks, and now bordering sections of the Hana Highway.

Brilliant red, pink and white **SPIDER LILIES** *(Crinum asiaticum)*, flowering year-round, brighten the park entrance. Smell their enticing fragrance, but please leave for others to enjoy.

Resembling a curved, pendant strand of pink-and-white porcelain shells, the **SHELL GINGER'S** *(Alpinia zerumbet)* blossoms emerge from tall, closely-packed leaf-blades. These artfully arranged floral necklaces should be just about at eye level as you take a quick spin to the bathrooms.

HONOMANU BAY

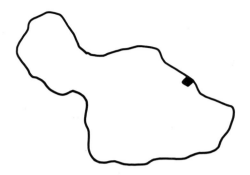

in the highway turn this into one of the most scenic spots on Maui. Drive slowly and carefully. Bask in its beauty! Incidentally, if you are tempted to complain about the condition of the road, just ask anyone what it was like before 1984, and you'll quickly extol its present virtues.

Snaking eastward the Hana Highway clings tenuously to precipitous 300 foot sea-cliffs, the highest you will encounter along the entire highway. Soon the large and U-shaped Honomanu Bay ("shark bay" pron. "Honno-ma-noo") indents the verdantly palisaded coastline by approximately one-third of a mile. Inland, coastal and seaward views from the numerous serpentine bends

One of the better vantage points lies on the Hana side of the bay as the road ascends from the gravelly flats, hugging the verdant mountainside. When the sun is shining the sea glitters far below; you may see blue-gray waters dappled by raindrops, but it's still lovely. A few pullouts allow space for a few cars enabling you to jump out and enjoy a **WESTWARD PERSPECTIVE OF HONOMANU** and its adjacent sea-cliffs.

The first view of Honomanu's sparkling waters, terminating in a surf-pounded bouldery beach, is breathtaking. Unfortunately it is an awkward place to stop your car. So immense is the valley ahead (it is the second biggest on Haleakala's north slope; the largest is at Ke'anae, just beyond) that it is still deep and difficult for back-packers to cross it at 7000' elevation, above timberline! Within a mile you will be practically at sea-level, as the road is forced to descend onto Honomanu Stream's broad flat, alluviated valley bottom close to its outlet. From the wave-washed beach and stream estuary (complete with a natural children's paddling pool on the Kahului side) you are graphically reminded that the Hana Highway is indeed skirting the flanks of a steep mountainside, with plenty of air and jagged rocks below the outer road edge. Perhaps by now you are wondering why the road is called a "highway."

Vegetation luxuriates, bursting forth from every rock, and crevice, reaching ever upwards for maximum sunlight in this huge **SHADY RAVINE.** Especially prominent are the pale-foliaged *kukui* trees (old friends by now) and the fiery red African tulip tree. The valley's slopes loom precipitously up to 1200′ on either side, containing the oldest exposed rocks on Haleakala. Stream erosion has gouged out a canyon so rugged that, even two and one-half miles inland, where it swells into a massive amphitheater, an inaccessible waterfall, the greatest of Honomanu's stepping-stone falls, thunders 400 feet into a mighty gulch. (Most of this water is, remember, tapped to irrigate sugar and pineapple fields, hence the meager flow at Honomanu's outlet).

Globes of frilly, tulip-shaped flowers, resembling lopsided cups of molten steel, protrude boldly from the **AFRICAN TULIP TREE'S** *(Spathodea campanulata)* dark green, compound-leaved foliage. Budding off from a central mass of curved brown buds, rings of these odd-shaped, scarlet-orange flowers (completely unrelated to "real tulips") crown the trees year-round. Originally from Africa, this showy ornamental has escaped from cultivation but is not a serious pest. Its flaming flashes provide a welcome addition to the multi-hued greens so characteristic of this lush coast.

Huge **"ELEPHANT EARS,"** thriving along the roadsides, are called 'ape (pronounced "ah-pay," not "ape") *Alocasia macrorrhiza*. They are closely related to taro, from which *poi* is made. If you peer under their shiny, dark, heart-shaped leaves, you may see some elegant cream flowers (right) reminiscent of anthuriums or calla lilies. Only eaten in times of extreme famine, this Asian-Polynesian introduction to Hawaii is *not edible*. It will greatly irritate your digestive system and throat membranes if treated like "regular" taro.

Common roadside doves are the **CHINESE SPOTTED DOVE** (*Streptopelia chinensis*, larger) and **ZEBRA DOVE** (*Geopelia striata*, smaller), both Asian escapees from captivity.

KEʻANAE
A. KEʻANAE ARBORETUM

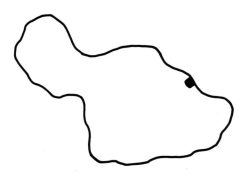

If you enjoy tropical verdure, this lush, free botanical garden, maintained by the DLNR, is worth a visit. It exhibits dozens of labelled, ornamental flowering and fruiting trees, palms, shrubs, gingers and heliconias, plus a whole section devoted to Polynesian-introduced plants such as taro, breadfruit, bananas, *ti*, sugar cane and *wauke* (from which bark cloth, tapa, was made). All planted in an essentially flat area, it is beautiful and educational.

For the more adventurous stroller, a roughish mile-long hike ascends *mauka* from the rear of the arboretum. It criss-crosses a rivulet and ascends through a mixture of native and planted vegetation up to a large forested flat. **This hike does not require permission. Permission for access into Maui's genuine rain forests, from any elevation, is difficult. Contacts are EMI, ranch managers, hunting clubs and numerous private landowners.**

Keʻanae weather is one of extremes. You may encounter muggy sunshine, pouring rain or both within a remarkably short span of time. Don't wander far from your car without raingear and a plastic bag to shield your camera in case you become caught in one of its frequent sudden downpours. One rule in tropical areas exceeding 100 inches of annual rainfall is: never trust the sun to keep shining!

Reminiscent of double rows of brilliantly painted bird's beaks, **HANGING LOBSTER CLAW'S** (*Heliconia rostrata*) two-dimensional, pendant flowers will visually magnetize any casual stroller through the arboretum.

(Opposite page) Right at the apex of a shaded hairpin turn, just past the YMCA Camp Ke'anae and before the turnoff to Ke'anae Village and the peninsula's lava shores, lies a large aluminum gate leading into the **KE'ANAE AR-BORETUM.** A stream bed with papaya trees, guavas and 'ape (huge taro-like leaves) on one side, and banks of colorful impatiens and ferns on the other, lines the easy path that leads to a well-tended profusion of native and introduced plants in a setting reminiscent of ancient times.

The palm exhibit includes several species of Maui's own rare **NATIVE PALMS** (*lo'ulu, Pritchardia* species). Their finely pleated leaves, downy gray beneath, do not shed fibers at their tips, a distinguishing feature from Chinese fan palms, common garden and hotel ornaments.

RED GINGERS (*Alpinia purpurata*), with their upright crimson floral heads, are real dazzlers, especially in the sunshine. Blooming throughout the year, this plant is unusual in that instead of liberating seeds, the mature flower-head sprouts dozens of leafy seedlings right where it bloomed.

A strikingly beautiful tree, the **BREADFRUIT** (*'ulu, Artocarpus altilis*), is unquestionably one of the most well-known Pacific trees (remember "Mutiny on the *Bounty*"?) and one of the world's truly great trees in terms of beauty, utility and cultural associations. Its foot-long, glossy leaves with their deeply indented lobes, resemble huge leathery hands. And its pale green fruits, the size of an infant's head, are formed from hundreds of individual flowers, much like a pineapple. Breadfruit is edible when cooked, but is not to everyone's taste. Deep-fried "chips" or thin slices of semi-ripe fruits, sauteed in butter and garlic, are palate pleasers. Note the sticky white sap, used in olden days for caulking canoes.

Eventually gravity drags these fast-growing plantlets towards the ground, whence they root beside their parent. Nearby is a fine grove of torch gingers (page 28).

"HAWAIIAN SUGARCANE"

(ko, Saccharum officinarum), introduced almost 1500 years ago by early Polynesian settlers, was the sweetest item in their diet until Captain Cook arrived in 1778. At Keanae are displayed several old varieties which have more colorful stalks and contain less fibrous matter than commercial sugar.

TARO *(Colocasia esculentum)* was, and still is, of deep spiritual and cultural significance to native Hawaiians. From its time of Polynesian introduction into Hawaii around 400 A.D., it branched into almost 200 different varieties, many of which have been preserved at Ke'anae. Note their imaginative names: a black-stalked green-leaved one is *hapu'u* (from its resemblance to *hapu'u* treeferns), and a stripey-stalked one is *manini*, recalling the pattern on the reef fish with the same name. The layout of taro patches, the irrigation system and bananas growing on upraised earth banks, are all features gleaned from ancient Polynesia. The blue-gray, floating fern is a recent innovation, cutting weeding time drastically.

The Arboretum houses a fine variety of **BANANAS** *(ma'ia, Musa paradisiaca),* both edible and ornamental. Bananas were originally brought to the islands by early Polynesian voyagers, but were never relied upon as staple foods unlike the rest of the Pacific. In fact (with few exceptions), if an Hawaiian woman was caught eating a banana she was severely punished, perhaps even killed.

B. KE'ANAE PENINSULA

According to Hawaiian legend Ke'anae Peninsula (pron. *"Kay-a-nigh"*) was the first spot on Maui to be blessed with water. In the days when the great gods of creation, Kane and Kanaloa, first inhabited these islands, the land was perfectly dry. However, on one particular visit to Ke'anae, Kane, with a Moses-style flourish of power, thrust his wooden staff into solid rock and water gushed forth! Since that moment Ke'anae (literally, "inheritance from heaven") and water have been inseparable companions.

Geologically too, Ke'anae is outstanding. Immense lava flows spewed out from Haleakala's massive caldera, and clunked down 9000' of elevation, eventually spilling into the ocean, creating a new peninsula that even today seems composed of "recent lava." Imagine clouds of hissing, super-heated steam rising into the air as this fiery molten rock, fresh from the bowels of the earth, tumbled uncontrollably into the Pacific's cool waters. If you can spare a few minutes, stop at the Wailua Wayside Overlook (main road, 0.4 mi. east of the Ke'anae Village turnoff). This points your eyes *mauka* to view this huge, ancient, cliff-flanked lava pathway, Ko'olau Gap, now almost completely vegetated. The trail and steps to this lookout, incidentally, enable you to pass through a tangled *hau* thicket (page 18), well-maintained for your convenience . . . watch the mossy, somewhat slippery steps.

There are few accessible spots in the Hawaiian Islands that rival the physical beauty and Polynesian charm provided by Ke'anae. (To locals, it's mighty good fishing here too!)

As we watch the powerful waves crashing against Ke'anae's crinkly black, jagged rocks, we sense a renewed awareness of Maui's recent volcanic origins. (The entire island, geologists inform us, is only 0.4-1.3 million years old.) This rough, **CLINKERY SUR-FACED LAVA** is one of Hawaii's two major lava types, *a'a* (pronounced "ah-ah"). The other,

pahoehoe (pronounced "pah-hoy-hoy"), smooth-surfaced and ropey, is best seen at Hawaii Volcanoes National Park on the Big Island. Watch your children here, especially if they are wearing sandals: it's easy to slip and graze hands and knees. Notice the few animals in Hawaii's tide-pools as compared to temperate sea-shores.

PI'INA'AU STREAM pours through several sections and plunge pools into Ko'olau Gap.

(Opposite page) Visible from the rim of Haleakala on a clear day, **KE'ANAE'S WAVE-THRASHED SHORES** can be discerned as a small white curve. Hiking up here at 7,000-8,900' is slow and tedious. The steep terrain, a jumbled mass of "topo-graphical inconveniences"—deep gullies, waterfalls, sheer rock cliffs, slippery streams and blind ridges—averages 25 gullies every contour mile, a challenge to even experienced woodsmen.

TARO'S large, attractive, arrow-headed leaves lend a rural, timeless Polynesian quality to the cultivated farmlands that comprise the bulk of Ke'anae's flatlands, which provide the bulk of Maui's fresh *poi*. Relished by Hawaiians, but not suited to all palates, *poi* is

manufactured from boiled, mashed and fermented taro "roots." Lowland taro, like rice, needs periodic monitoring of water levels to grow to perfection. Within the colorful patchwork quilt of taro fields, one can identify its various growth stages: fallow ground (brown, no water), freshly planted baby taro (tiny plants dotting a shallow pond), young taro (pale green with shallow water), and mature plants ready for harvest (dark green, no water visible). Coconuts and bananas, integrated into these traditional wetland agricultural practices, benefit from the ever-flowing irrigation channels.

Serving a close-knit community of extended families, the **KE'ANAE CONGREGATIONAL CHURCH** is an historic landmark, having reposed near the peninsula's tip since 1860. Its cool stone walls enclose an unpretentious but special chapel laid with locally woven *hala* floor coverings. Outside, graceful coconuts, well-maintained lawns and gardens add additional charm. To generate a feeling for the Hawaiians, their names and ways, visit the tiny cemetery.

A **PARROT'S BEAK HELI-CONIA** *(Heliconia psittacorum)* with its orange "parrot-like" floral parts, can be seen in Ke'anae gardens.

GARDENS are neat, colorful and well-tended in Ke'anae Village, despite the humid climate (which encourages rapid growth) and a constantly windy, salty atmosphere. Most residents are of Hawaiian descent, living a partly self-sufficient life-style. The nearest stores are nearly 30 miles back at Pa'ia or the same distance ahead to Hana.

The elegant, scissor-tailed silhouettes of **GREAT FRIGATE-BIRDS** *(Fregata minor),* known locally as *'iwa* (pronounced "ee-va") can generally be spotted soaring effortlessly above the Ke'anae coast. Sexes are easy to distinguish: males are all-black, females are black with white breasts, and juveniles are black with white breasts and heads. Utilizing warm thermal currents, the slender, agile *'iwa* spiral (usually without flapping) hundreds of feet upwards. Though only three and a half feet long, with a seven-foot wingspan, these primitive seabirds are the original "featherweights": their feathers weigh the same amount as their bones, approximately 4 ounces!

Munch on your **PICNIC LUNCH IN A SIMPLE PACIFIC ISLAND SETTING.** This will be an hour you will remember, so never mind the strong breeze. *Hala* trees, considered a nature spirit in old Hawaii, have provided materials for housing, clothing, food, medicine, ornaments, fishing implements and religious rituals for centuries. Notice the spirally tufted leaves and root-stilts. When its leaves are de-spined (watch your fingers) and dried they are woven into esthetically pleasing, durable **HALA MATS.**

This traditional Polynesian art is still (barely) alive. Old mats can be seen in the nearby Ke'anae Congregational Church.

A gorgeous **WESTWARD VIEW OF COASTLINE** adjacent to Ke'anae, through a false kamani tree (*Terminalia catappa*).

Beautiful **STORM SURF,** of common occurence, during late afternoon at Ke'anae Peninsula.

A haven for seabirds, **MOKU MANA ISLET** looms straight and high enough to defy human interference (except from helicopters, which is illegal). Part of Maui's offshore island refuge system, Moku Mana offers protected status to beautiful tropical seabirds such as the Great Frigatebird, White-tailed Tropicbird, Wedge-tailed Shearwater and Hawaiian Noddy Terns. Access is difficult because of private land-holdings.

Steady tradewinds from the north-east, bringing about 150 inches of rain annually, and powerful surf, have eroded Ke'anae's coastline into some fantastic shapes. **MOKU MANA** (literally "life spirit of the birds") and **MANAHOA** ("Needle") **ROCK** are framed within a natural sea-arch at Pauwalu Point, one-half mile east of Ke'anae.

43

WAILUA TO PUA'A KA'A

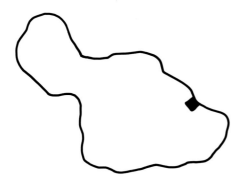

If you enjoy waterfalls, slow down for this section of the road. Twisting and turning, the road climbs back up to 1275 feet, crossing more gullies. Water streams in every conceivable manner above and below the next few miles of highway including terracing cascades, "bridal veils," long skinny falls or just "plain" ones. Each time you encounter them they are different! Nature provides the most ideal viewing conditions when the sun shines after heavy rain, although at any time they are stunning. Remember — the more rain, the more water and the more exquisite the falls.

When rains begin to erode fresh terrain, the first changes to appear are rills, fissures, and clefts created by swift-flowing streams. As time progresses, these channels enlarge into gulches, chasms, ravines, gullies, valleys, gorges and eventually canyons. As Haleakala continues its ever-changing land-sculpturing, which results in myriads of valleys, ridges, waterfalls, and sea-cliffs we, as temporary or permanent visitors to this lovely island, are privileged to witness its evolution. In a mere 15 million years Maui will have disappeared forever under this aqueous onslaught!

A scenic waterfall, **KOPILIULA STREAM,** adjacent to the highway.

There have always been ample rains in this area. The Hawaiians, sensitive to even minute changes in weather, composed many chants related to wind and rain:

"'Twas in Ko'olau * I met with the
  rain;
It comes with the lifting and tossing
  of dust,
Advancing in columns, dashing
  along,
The rain, it sighs in the forest . . .
It smites, it smites now the land . . .
Full run the streams, a rushing
  flood;
The mountain walls leap with the
  rain."

*Specifically the large valley above the Ke'anae Peninsula; generally, the rain forest encompassing most of Haleakala's northern slopes.

Do you wonder what lies upslope? Here is a helicopter's eye view of a **CHAIN OF POOLS AND FALLS, WAILUANUI STREAM,** above the highway. Hawaii has so many waterfalls that most, such as these, are unnamed.

A nine-year old Mauian is excited on her first discovery of **WAIO-KUNA FALLS.**

WATERFALLS, gushing after heavy mountain rains, are always a thrill to encounter.

WAIKANI FALLS, fed by pure spring water, on two different trips. Note the wedding party's traditional **MAILE** leis.

Down at the coast, more **CAVES AND SEA-STACKS** dot the rugged coastline. This cave is accessible only by canoe through a "dragon's teeth" barricade of jagged rocks and tricky winds and swirling currents.

"OUR LADY OF FATIMA SHRINE," built in 1860, lends a quaint charm to the tiny village of Wailua. The total population of Wailua and its sister village, Ke'anae, is about 250.

Wailua (pron. "Why-loo-ah"), like Ke'anae, boasts impeccably tended gardens that radiate color. **BOUGAINVILLEA (***Bougainvillea* species) a woody vine that is grown extensively in all tropical, subtropical and warm-temperate areas, calls Brazil its "real home." It needs full sunlight, warm year-round temperatures, and heavy pruning to maintain its brilliance, which comes in shades of magenta, purple, yellow, orange, pink and white. Notice that the true flowers (small and white), nestle amongst wide collars of colorful bracts (modified leaves). As in heliconias, the bright color that first attracts one's eye comes from the unusual *leaves* rather than *flowers*. Watch out for its spines, especially when bare-footed!

PUA'A KA'A TO NAHIKU

Pua'a Ka'a State Park (pron. "Poo-*ah*-ah *Kah*-ah") makes a delightful stopping spot. Its name, literally translated, means "Park of the Rolling Pigs." Heliconias, gingers, tree-ferns, guavas and native trees all vie for space in the rangy lushness of this small garden-cum-park. Complete with a trickling stream meandering through its lawns, picnic tables, pools and waterfalls on two levels, it is very different from a regular picnic ground. Children can watch tadpoles and baby frogs writhing and jumping about in the shallow pools. Note the lack of safety railings and stay close to your little ones.

This stretch of highway, moving in part through native forests, hovers around the 1200 feet, the highest elevation we encounter on our circumnavigatory excursion of Haleakala, until we reach Kula on the dry, western side. Here the EMI ditches are easily seen. One parallels the road, giving us a glimpse of the immense quantities of water that are shunted from mountain to lowland to irrigate pineapples and sugar.

If you've been counting bridges since Haiku, you're adding quite a few now. Some gulches are so narrow bridging hardly seems necessary, but look how deep and ominous the clefts below are!

Three hillocks *(pu'u)* between 1800 and 3200 feet scallop Nahiku's horizon on an exceptionally clear day. The ever-present **SWORD FERNS** *(Nephrolepis exaltata)* grow thick and tall in the foreground.

sometimes wildly, through precipitous, bouldery gullies and fairylands of ferns and mosses, eventually to be augmented by several huge, cold underground springs below the highway. In a mighty outburst of energy it thunders over a 200 foot precipice before emptying into the ocean at Nahiku. Note the difference in water volume between the waterfalls on the highway (left) and downstream, less than one mile distant (below and back cover).

HANAWI STREAM, a name familiar to Mauians, was the focus of a controversial conservation issue around 1980. The last of East Maui's streams untapped for irrigation below the Hana Highway, it has become a solace for native and endangered species of fish *(o'opu)* and a shrimp *(opae)* that, like salmon, need to travel to the ocean and back to complete their breeding cycle. Its steep, heavily wooded and impassable drainage system contains many scenic gems worthy of National Park status. From its source as a rounded depression at high elevations, it travels, sometimes gently,

STORM CLOUDS gather over Haleakala's slopes above Pua'a Ka'a State Park close to Haleakala's rim. Rain gauge readings from this section of the mountain average 390 inches annually, at times exceeding 500 inches. This makes it the second wettest area in Hawaii and one of the soggiest in the world. No wonder there are so many waterfalls!

The **SMALL INDIAN MONGOOSE** *(Herpestes auropunctatus)* is an introduced, brown, weasel-like pest which has exterminated all Hawaii's ground-nesting birds (it is present on all islands except Kauai). It is sometimes called a "squeasel"—a cross between a squirrel and a weasel! Pua'a Ka'a trash cans are a prime spot to see them.

'OHI'A LEHUA *(Metrosideros collina)* is Hawaii's major forest tree. With its twisted gray trunks, small rounded leaves and gay red pompons, it dominates Maui's craggy mountains and valleys, producing a uniquely Hawaiian forest. At Pua'a Ka'a we skirt the lower edge of the *'ohi'a lehua* forest, part of the enormous Ko'olau Forest Reserve. However, few of the State's forests are pristine. The sickly *'ohi'a* trees that you pass suffer from a little-understood, much-studied phenomenon termed *"'ohi'a*-dieback."

The curved leaves and wide-spreading branches of Hawaii's famous native **KOA** *(Acacia koa)* tree occur commonly near Pua'a Ka'a. *Koa* forests, though diminishing rapidly, are still felled to make furniture, ukuleles and prized bowls. Its reddish, mahogany-like wood contains beautifully flowing, variegated grains. *Koa* is sometimes confused with Australian eucalyptus, which also possess curved leaves.

Native birds are mostly restricted to *'ohi'a lehua* forests above the 4000 foot elevation beyond the limits of mosquitos. These little devils that bite you in Hawaii's lowlands carry "bird malaria," similar to human malaria, which restricts bird distribution. Most birds you see in Hawaii have been introduced from elsewhere, such as the **JAPANESE WHITE-EYE** *(Zosterops japonicus)*, left, commonly called *mejiro* by Japanese residents, and the **NORTHERN CARDINAL** *(Cardinalis cardinalis)*, center, familiar to all mainlanders.

WAIANAPANAPA

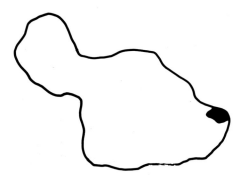

Waianapanapa (pron. "Why-ah-*nah*-pa-*nah*-pa") State Park, is yet another interesting stop en route to Hana, providing picnicking, camping (State DLNR permits are required in advance) and hiking facilities. Its ruggedly scenic cliffs of crinkly black lava flanked by thick native coastal forest, offer a unique experience for those who have extra hours. However, it is not a place to rush in and out in ten minutes.

Here 120 acres have been preserved by the State of Hawaii, not only for their natural beauty but for the numerous historical sites — walls, house foundations, *heiau* (temples) and gravesites — that are sprinkled over a relatively small area. Loose-stoned walls abound here, marking locations of domestic and religious significance. Beneath raised platforms topped with smooth boulders lie human bones that are still respected by today's Hawaiians. They are not play areas for children!

Elemental water music is strong here. The pounding thumps of tumultuous swells battering against perforated cliff-faces provide a *basso continuo* for the intermittent swishes of foam lurching up Pa'iloa's black sand beach, the whooshing waters channeling within rocky intersties, and the ejaculatory hisses of blowholes.

Superimposed upon these marine utterances are wild cries of Noddy Terns, rattling *hala* leaves, pouring rain (short, heavy showers are common) and perhaps within Waianapanapa's early morning stillness, the gentle purring of your own heartbeat.

Accessible only by canoe, **SEA-ARCHES, BASALTIC COLUMNS AND CAVES** fascinate adventurous explorers.

Down the bumpy, muddy Ulaino road lies Maui's largest ancient temple site, **PI'ILANIHALE HEIAU**, now on the National Register of Historic Sites. Built entirely from surrounding lava rocks, this massive structure has dimensions which rival the biggest sites in Hawaii. The Pacific Tropical Botanical Garden has landscaped the area beautifully, including the building of a shelter with a delightful coastal view through spirals of *hala* leaves (bottom right). Not open to public.

The **ULAINO SHORELINE** from offshore.

If you swim at the wave-worn, black pebbly beach at Pa'iloa Bay (below the campground), watch for small, blue **PORTUGUESE MAN-O-WAR** "bladders" *(Physalia)* that tend to congregate here. Sometimes the water is so dense with them that, after even a quick dip, your skin may feel prickly stings for hours. For some reason, these little colonial floaters are quite consistent here and rarely a problem elsewhere in the islands. Reasonable numbers of reef-fish occur here, although there is no coral. Snorkeling should only be tackled by experienced swimmers.

53

A labyrinth of eroded lava-tubes, natural arches and irregular islets lie along the **PICTURESQUE WAIANAPANAPA COAST.** Surging waves constantly crash against the jagged rocks, furthering the process of erosion. Their booming is particularly dramatic during storms.

Swells surge into the multi-entranced **CAVE SYSTEM** at Ulaino.

The delectable perfume of **PLUMERIAS** *(Plumeria spp)* bespeak the "romantic tropics." For many of us the first wiff of these simple but irresistible yellow and white blossoms created a memory that has not yet faded. Plumeria trees are dotted around the park for all to enjoy (pluck one if you wish. Boys—pop one behind your special girl's ear, the right ear if she is "taken," the left if she's "available.") Smell them at dawn, dusk or during mid-day heat; they will never disappoint you.

54

Forests of *hala*, bordered with the bright green native succulent **BEACH NAUPAKA** *(Scaevola taccada)*, enhance the pristine beauty of this Pacific-looking area. Naupaka's pithy, white seeds, dubbed "hailstones" in the Hawaiian language, possess remarkable tolerance to salt. They can germinate even after one year of immersion in salt water!

The **FRESH-WATER CAVES** of Waianapanapa can be reached by a short (but somewhat slippery) loop trail from the upper parking lot. Damp, mossy and luxuriant, the cave area, actually a collapsed lava tube, contains two pools, both colored red from thousands of tiny shrimp that crawl in their shallows. The first pool is a reminder of the princess' blood; the second is the site of a long-gone bloody fight between a chief and his unfaithful wife; you can read about it on the wooden sign at the trail entrance.

JAGGED COASTAL ROCKS AND ISLANDS enhance the edge of Waianapanapa's picnic and camping areas.

STONE OFFERINGS are sacred. Please respect them. It is considered inappropriate for visitors to build *ahu* (rock piles) or wrap *ti* leaves around rocks.

Cultivated varieties of **TI** thrive in this hot, humid climate. Those with variegated red-purple leaf-blades and scarlet seeds are popular in gardens.

A dark brown inshore seabird with long slender wings and snowy crown flies close to you as you stand on the cliffs or swim in the water. Suddenly it flutters then swoops gracefully down to snap up a fish. These 14-inch long terns are called by a variety of names: Hawaiian, White-capped or **BLACK NODDY TERNS** (or Noddies), *Anous minutus*.

The easy, three-mile **WAIANA-PANAPA COASTAL TRAIL,** part of the ancient *alaloa* ("long trail") that originally extended around the entire island coastline, begins near the caretaker's home, closely follows the cliff-edge and ends in Hana. Don't worry about getting sprayed occasionally. Keep to the trail to avoid grazing your toes or twisting your ankles. Tennis shoes or boots are best. Beneath your feet run a honeycomb of erratic tunnels and gaping pits caused by gases becoming trapped under cooling lava, and evidenced by sounds of rushing water. Not far in the Hana direction (east) lies a blowhole and *heiau* with stone offerings. In the opposite direction from the park lies another cliffside trail (one mile long) to Hana airport, along which lie ancient, raised gravesites.

HANA

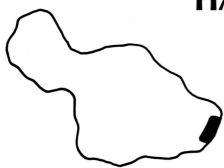

Hana—a special place. It's the most isolated, most tropical, most laid-back, most muggy, most friendly, most "real Hawaiian" community on Maui.

In the early morning you can watch the sunrise develop in both directions as the mountain clouds catch the dawn hues from the eastern sun. Rain pelts you when you barely noticed a cloud in the sky. Whales spout offshore and long ribbons of water plunge down precipitous valley walls. Lone fishermen on rocky points throw circular fishnets into choppy blue water. You can pull sizeable weeds that you swear were not in your garden two days ago, and pick plumerias all-year.

Hana (pron. "Ha-nah") is a place to imbibe Nature's bounteous gifts and glimpse snatches of past Polynesian civilization. Its congenial, take-your-time ambience is very relaxing.

What, you ask, do people *do* here? They fish, hunt pigs in the forested valleys, grow flowers, raise children, help one another. They work in the hospital, hotels, stores, schools, on roads, or for the National Park Service.

During off-hours they love to eat, sing, dance, have fun, drink beer, string leis, and "talk story" (pidgin for gab).

Hana's horizons are circumscribed. Activities revolve around the weather and what people feel like doing. You don't have to apologize if you show up late . . . or not at all. Life flows pretty smoothly just as it has for centuries. But if a valid controversial issue arises "on the other side" (i.e. anywhere else on Maui) that may affect Hana residents, some will jump up and become involved. Their way of life means a lot to them, and the community association is the most active on Maui.

Hana residents are incredibly diverse. You have the locals, most of Hawaiian extraction, whose "roots" extend back generations; and the haoles, many of whom have been influential during their careers. The residuum includes leftovers from the 1960's "hippie" era, television personalities and even an ex-Broadway-cum-opera singer. They range from living in luxury to eking out a simple existence from little plots of land.

However, Hana does an admirable job of pleasing everyone. Take music. Hana people love it. Radio reception is poor, so they turn to live music. Guitars and ukuleles suffice for most, but for the classically-minded, Hana doesn't do too badly. Periodic concerts (some from world-class musicians) are provided by the Maui Philharmonic Society and for several years there was a dear old lady (ex-Chicago) who held "record concerts." One could hear "The Messiah" or esoteric chamber music, all in living room comfort, complete with a cup of hot tea!

Kindness, friendliness and co-operation are alive and well in this gentle rural outpost. Residents, of whatever background, share three attributes: happiness, a "plenty-of-time" attitude and aloha. But aloha *may* become old with approximately one-half million people driving by each year. So let your pace be unhurried, your smile genuine, and your behavior polite, so that Hana can remain that "extra special place" for others, and for you when you return.

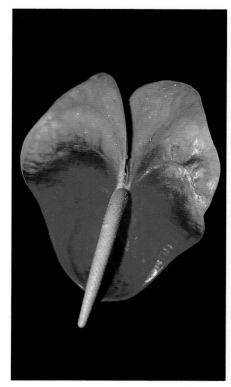

A gorgeous *obake* anthurium.

Delightfully lush landscaping at the **HOTEL HANA MAUI.**

expanse of lush, jungly, tropical vegetation (heliconias, gingers, palms, tall trees, etc.) the latter is especially recommended. Pictured are the ferny-foliaged **PINK** (left) and **RAINBOW** (right) **SHOWER TREES** (check out the Hana Medical Center), **RED-AND-YELLOW CANNAS** (bottom left), and the bountiful **RED HIBISCUS** (bottom right).

After a predominance of greenery encountered along the highway thus far, Hana abounds with color. Its gentle muggy breezes waft garden smells all around; Hana and flowers are inseparable companions. Gardens and nurseries (nominal admission) such as Hana Gardenland and Helani Gardens are well worth a visit. If you are looking for a large

One of Hana's reliable rains is the *apuakea*. Falling right after sunrise, it sweeps inland from the ocean, drenching everything and everybody in its inexorable path. Skies turn a clean whitish-gray and Hana becomes bathed in a clear yellow dawn light, reminiscent of high latitude regions such as Alaska or Scotland. These **PASTURE COCONUTS** were photographed around 6 a.m. between several bouts of pouring rain and blinks of sun.

Keenly attuned to slight weather changes, ancient Hawaiians named hundreds of localized breezes, winds and rains: "short, sharp winds," "dust-driven winds," "wind-mist clouds," "pelting rains," etc.

No trip to Hana is complete without at least noticing the famous **HASEGAWA STORE.** Somewhat a legend (even immortalized in song), this aloha-filled, delightfully overflowing country store (begun in 1910) is designed to carry everything you need plus incidentals to interest the visitor. If you need film, 2x4's, beer or diapers, Harry the friendly proprietor, is bound to stock it.

Hana residents take pride in their gardens, whose upkeep often occupies a good percentage of their recreational time. Don't be fooled by their neatness. . . . gardening in wet, tropical areas requires constant weeding, extensive trimming and heavy pruning. A dear friend once exclaimed to us: "O, how wonderful, weeds don't even grow in Paradise!" Such thoughts are impractical. This charming home has a front hedge of **MEXI-CAN CREEPER** or "chain of love" (*Antigonon leptopus*), a trailing vine covered with bunches of little pink floral hearts.

ALAU ISLAND, a quarter mile offshore from Hamoa Beach Road, sits on the far side of a treacherous, rocky channel. Notice the extensive area of white water around it, a warning sign that even closer to where you are standing, rip-currents and exposed rocks make swimming unsafe. Its 150-foot summit, crowned by two coconut palms, occasionally gets sprayed by crashing waves.

Hana is a very social place; it is a rural community, with regular meetings and numerous activities that involve large groups of people. Most weekends provide excuses for a celebration — baby's first birthday, anniversaries, weddings, etc. Hana residents love to get together and have fun catching pigs, fish and crabs, netting shrimps, and pounding poi for *luau*. Shown is the **WEDDING OF SAM & BECKY KALALAU,** St. Mary's Church, 1980.

Tucked within semi-circular Mokae Cove lies **HAMOA BEACH,** a beautiful, restful spot maintained by the famous Hotel Hana Maui, with public access and shower. It's a good place to jump in the surf, swim, or just lie in the sun (or rain — hardly a day passes without some rain.)

Churches are important focal points of social life in Hana. The Congregational **WANANA-LUA CHURCH** (center of town), built in 1838, has immaculate landscaping and a spacious, acoustically excellent, wooden interior.

"TROPICALS:" HELICONIAS, GINGERS AND TROPICAL FOLIAGE are a booming cut-flower business in Hana. Growers can barely keep pace with the national and international demand for these stunning flowers and leaves. Tours of the major farm, Ali'i Gardens, can be arranged. Pictured is Indonesian wax ginger (*Tapeinochilus ananassae*).

A few residential streets comprising the **SMALL TOWN OF HANA** (population 1200 from Ke'anae to Kaupo) are grouped around **HANA BAY**. A nice over-view of green pastures and distant town, can be obtained by driving up to the stone cross (a memorial to Paul Fagan, remembered most for opening Hana to tourism). Bask in the quietness, simplicity and fresh air.

Resembling a long-necked bird with crest, each **BIRD-OF-PARADISE** (*Strelitzia reginae*) blends full color, classic poise and floral self-assur-ance. What perfection of line . . . what exoticism! Arising from a boat-shaped, basal sheath, up to six dazzling flowers emerge over a week or two in a sunburst of glossy orange and blue. Year-round beauties, they occur on Maui not only in their natural state but in many artistic guises: quilts, stained glass, paintings, bags, silk clothing and even logos for windsurfers.

HANA BAY: a destination spot for millions of tourists.

ANTHURIUMS (*Anthurium andraeanum*), today symbols of tropical island elegance, are not native to Hawaii, but originated in Colombia, South America.

Denizens of muggy rainforests, they are at home perching on branches amidst the dense shade of multilayered tiers of lush vegetation. All commercial anthuriums in the State are grown on the Big Island, whose humid, frequently drizzly, gray climate provides ideal growing conditions. However, residents of muggy areas such as Hana, grow them for pleasure. They thrive under tree-ferns.

ORCHIDS. Exquisite, gorgeous, elegant . . . . Mere mention of these symbols of floral excellence conjures visions of far-away lush rainforests, hobbyists trekking through humid jungles, expensive florists and beautiful places like Hana. Look around in people's gardens and you'll see some, but do not expect fancy orchids to dangle from forest verdure. For reasons related to isolation in the middle of a huge ocean, Hawaii harbors few native species; none are ravishing beauties.

KIPAHULU

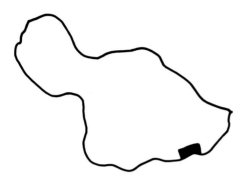

Kipahulu (pron. "Key-pah-*hoo*-loo"): its dripping lushness, beauty, isolation and grandeur are personal experiences. Feel its salty air; become drenched, laughingly, in its torrential rains; taste its scrumptious papayas; wonder at its waterfalls; smell its perfumy, dank air; relish its riot of color in rambly gardens and jungly verdure; and marvel at its unconquerable precipices. Humans here are mere observers of the powerful elemental forces that have shaped, and will continue to shape Maui for millenia.

For those interested in hiking, a very rewarding **HALF-MILE WALK** is a stroll from the parking lot through undulating, guava-studded pastures leading to the splendid falls at Makahiku and on to Waimoku Falls (in distance).

THE FALLS AT MAKAHIKU plunges 185 feet into one of 'Ohe'o Gulch's many turbulent pools. STAY BEHIND THE RAIL; the cliff is undercut and vertically precipitous. Near here an overzealous lady once ended up dangling precariously on the cliff-face 30 feet below its rim, requiring a helicopter with suspended rangers to pluck off her mangled body. Such risky maneuvers are hazardous for both parties.

Familiar to all Kipahulu travelers are the much-photographed **WAILUA FALLS** (lit. "two waters"), named for the two streams that flow into Wailua Cove below. Undoubtedly the most attractive of Maui's accessible waterfalls, this 100 foot beauty is generally viewed from a concrete bridge through handsome breadfruit leaves. Beneath the maple-leaved *kukui* trees grow lush torch gingers. A short (but slippery), muddy trail leads to the base of the Falls, providing a showery, but magnificent, exposure to their power. On returning to your car (especially if you are caught in clogged traffic; delays may reach 30 minutes), peer down the chasm below the bridge. Hang onto little hands!

Lushness and wildness typify Kipahulu, whether the brightly colored **TOUCH-ME-NOTS** (*Impatiens suttoni*) along the roadsides (left) or verdant **FOREST GREEN-ERY** at higher elevations. A native of the Malagasy Republic, these cheery impatiens have fat, ellipitical seedpods which children love to pop — hence their other name, "touch-me-not."

The **ROAD BEYOND HANA** resembles the entire highway "in the old days" (pre-1984). Prepare for jiggling stomachs and, during afternoon hours, plenty of oncoming traffic. Kipahulu is not "just around the corner" from Hana. It is a slow, windy, bumpy drive. Tiring but scenic, it requires the most driving concentration required yet. If you are tired or running out of time, buy an ice-cream in Hana and turn back. Rental cars are not permitted to drive past Kipahulu. Incidentally, if you want to take photos, please pull off the road so as not to block it.

Photos courtesy of NPS.

About 1000 feet from the Kipahulu Ranger Station toward the mouth of 'Ohe'o Stream the National Park Service (NPS) and residents of the Hana and Kipahulu area are building a Hawaiian Kauhale complex. A one-fourth size canoe shelter is finished. Other traditional thatched-roof Hawaiian structures planned include a full-size canoe shelter, sleeping structures for men and women, cook shelters, hula platform and related structures. The NPS will regularly present cultural demonstrations—check bulletin boards or stop by the Ranger Station for times and locations.

If you arrive at the famed
'OHE'O GULCH
(pron. "O-hay-o") during
a sunny spell, don't be alarmed if you are greeted by the sight of dozens of sun-bathers spread over the boulders. . . . in 1985, over 400,000 visitors crossed 'Ohe'o's bridge! A very worthwhile loop trail, an easy 0.6 mi., leads from the parking lot across pastures dotted with old house ruins, to the seashore, up beside five pools and falls (others lie above the bridge) and back to your car.

Pick up an informative leaflet from the National Park Service, and remember there are no life guards, so swimming in the pools is at your own risk. Unanticipated flooding and swift, swirling currents are highly dangerous, as are muddied waters and submerged rocks. NO DIVING IS PERMITTED. ON NO ACCOUNT SWIM IN THE OCEAN HERE.

Hundreds of cascading streams dot Haleakala's flanks; 'Ohe'o happens to be an accessible and especially lovely one. Actually, 'Ohe'o Stream has gouged out over 20 pools within its lowest mile, which prompted the original Hawaiian name, "the gathering of pools." In deference to the long standing heritage of this picturesque spot, the wishes of the National Park Service and local Hawaiians, please use the traditional name, 'Ohe'o.

PAPAYAS *(Carica papaya),* native to South America, were first brought to Hawaii in the early 1800's. Today these delectable fruits, along with plumerias, Vanda orchids, surfers and hula skirts, practically epitomize island life to the outsider. To be outstandingly tasty, papayas need to be tree-ripened at low elevations with plenty of sunshine and rain. These conditions are amply met with in Kipahulu, whose orchards provide fruit for markets "on the other side." Papaya plants come in three "sexes": male, female and herma-phrodite (both). Male trees have long-stemmed flower-clusters but produce no fruit, while female trees sprout flowers close to the stem, each of which matures into a round fruit. Hermaphrodites, the most desirable, bud off large quantities of the familiar, pear-shaped delicacies.

Kipahulu Valley, an isolated world in itself, extends from a broad lava fan near sea level between steep walls to a narrow pali (cliff) isolating it from Hale-akala. In early times, groups of extended families shared pie-shaped sections of land *(ahupua'a).* Beginning offshore (for fishing), these long-triangular land divisions extended inland through many elevations, enabling people to obtain or grow all the commodities necessary for simple living. This unusual **VIEW FROM KUKUI PEAK,** taken on an exceptionally clear day, looks across Kipahulu and Waihoi Valleys to distant Hana.

Whirling furiously through a narrow, meandering gorge, **PIPIWAI STREAM** hastens to meet the ocean at lower 'Ohe'o Gulch. Annual rainfall exceeds 200 inches here, so there is usually plenty of water to feed the water-courses, all sculpted deeply through the underlying lava. Right above here is the stream crossing leading to the spectacular, 385' high Waimoku Falls. DO NOT CROSS THE STREAM IF IT IS HIGH.

KIPAHULU CAMPGROUND, accessible by trail from the view shown, is undeveloped and rather primitive. Pitch your tent in the designated pasture and enjoy Nature: her spectacular, indented coastlines, cascades, pools, sea-breezes and rains. Chemical and pit-toilets and a few picnic tables are provided. No entrance or camping permits are necessary, although three days is the maximum length of stay. Remember about pig-pollution and erosion (page 26) and bring your own drinking water. WATER IS UNSAFE TO DRINK, causing a variety of disorders ranging from simple diarrhea to serious ghiardiasis and leptospirosis. In this aerial photo, the gulch with pools lies centrally.

EVENING CLOUDS coalesce and solidify in upper Kipahulu.

KIPAHULU'S OLD SUGAR MILL, with its 96-foot high smokestack, reminds us of flourish-ing, but difficult, times between 1881 and 1925, when sugar was big business here. Inconveniences galore beset the mill-operators: lack of roads and harbors; floods roar-ing through gullies washing away trails and bridges; and heavy rains muddying up fields and equipment. When sugar died, ranching became the main industry until the advent of tourism in the 1960's. You can still see old railroad tracks on the Hana pier.

Heavily wooded, craggy topography abounds here; a jumble of roughly broken slopes sweep ruggedly down to inaccessible seacliffs. Winding around one valley you pass a white cross, not

Lindbergh's, but **HELIO'S GRAVE.** Born on this island in 1815, Helio was Maui's first enthusiastic exponent of the Catholic faith, instructing 4000 people during his thirty-one year lifespan. Do not hike the trail by the information sign; it is treacherous.

CHARLES LINDBERGH, known to millions for his historic trans-Atlantic flight in 1927, flew in 1974 from a New York hospital to Hana to spend his last days in solitude with his family. Wracked with incurable cancer, he planned all the details of his simple funeral. A rough-hewn eucalyptus coffin, resting in the back of a local pickup truck, was his hearse. There is no sign to his resting-place. It is in a small church graveyard in Kipahulu. Those who wish to pay him their respects usually find him. A small donation to help maintain the church and grounds is always appreciated.

Weaving in and out of precipitous gulches, the highway bypasses seacliffs rising to 350 feet. This **COASTAL SECTION OF WAIHO'I VALLEY,** adjacent to Kipahulu, lies just south of Wailua Falls and Helio's grave.

An **OBLIQUE RIDGE** is all that divides upper Kipahulu Valley (left) from Haleakala (right).

The precipitous **HEADWALLS OF KIPAHULU VALLEY.**

Maui Parrotbill *(Pseudonestor xanthrophrys).*

A native lobelia *(Cyanea aculeatiflora).*

Mere mention of Kipahulu Valley to resident Mauians stirs thoughts of native rain forests harboring rare plants and birds. It is true. Since 1969, Haleakala National Park added the wet Kipahulu District (9,000 acres) to their dry Haleakala region, bringing the Park's total acreage to 28,655. Despite high populations of damaging, feral pigs (extensive management and fencing are currently underway), rugged **UPPER KIPAHULU VALLEY** still harbors avian rarities such as the **MAUI PARROTBILL** and native flowers such as **LOBELIAS, BEGONIAS** and **RARE GREENSWORDS** in remote foggy bogs. Such floral specialties are only seen by a handful of hardy biologists and National Park employees willing to get tired, wet and muddy for days on end.

A spiny, native lobelia *(Cyanea horrida).*

A greensword *(Argyroxiphium virescens)*, a bog relative of the famous crater silverswords.

A native begonia, *puamakanui (Hillebrandia sandwicensis)*.

A bounty of native forest ferns.

A stunning, candelabra-like lobelia, *koli'i (Trematolobelia macrostachys)*.

A close view of the splendid rosy flowers of *koli'i*.

BEYOND KIPAHULU

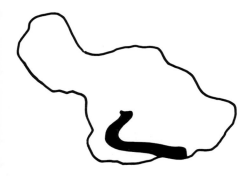

At Kipahulu, 99 percent of people turn their cars around and head back to Kahului. The road beyond is in such poor condition that it is often fit only for four-wheeled drive vehicles, pickups and high-slung vans. For hunters and other Mauians who are familiar with its hazards, this section is included. Storms and high waves can make it impassable for weeks.

Its many miles of "washboard dirt," passing through free-ranging cattle country, is desert-like (in places reminiscent of southeast Arizona) and virtually uninhabited. Traffic is sparse, there are no emergency telephones, no water, and the nearest mechanic is in Kula, many lonely miles distant. If your axle breaks or you run out of gasoline, it may well be the next morning before you can hope for help.

On reaching Kula, you drive through greenery of Australian black wattles and eucalyptus trees, interspersed with jacarandas and golden-flowered silk oaks. Temperate vegetables, fruits and flowers such as figs, avocados, peaches, carnations and proteas thrive here.

It is easy to envision how KAUPO GAP was formerly a deep, wide valley through which lava poured. A rough, dry, but well-trodden 7.7 mile hike connects Paliku Cabin in the eastern end of Haleakala, to Kaupo Village. This is the only trail from Haleakala down to any Maui coast.

HALEAKALA'S SOUTH SLOPE, in the rain-shadow of Maui's northeast tradewinds, was formerly clothed in native dryland forests. Now fissured with hundreds of dry gullies ranging from a few feet to over 200 feet deep, this area has been virtually destroyed by feral goats.

Crossing steep cliffs, a rustic road leads around **LELEKEA BAY** towards Maui's south side, which lies in the rain shadow of Haleakala. The loose, gravelly road (now no longer officially the Hana Highway but Kaupo Road), bounded on one side by rocky cliffs and on the other by an unrailed drop to the ocean, is so narrow in places that one needs to reverse small distances up or down to allow passage of oncoming cars.

HUIALOHA CHURCH, located on a rocky point, provides a windswept but shady picnic spot for hot, thirsty travelers or hikers. Within this "gathering place of love," with its unpretentious stone-walled chapel, a handful of Kaupo residents still worship. In 1976, during America's bicentennial celebrations, President Nixon had requested that every church bell in the nation be rung on July 4. Some Hana residents traveled out here, and with will power and muscular force, managed to budge this poor bell that had been rusted frozen for decades, restoring it to life. Distant photo shows its location on **MOKULAU PENINSULA** from an upslope ridge. Huialoha Church will soon be placed on the National Register of Historic Places.

Many **COASTAL HAWAIIAN VILLAGES** lie in deserted areas below the road. Mountain forests were formerly more extensive, streams flowed, and underground water-holes provided water for village inhabitants.

The *wiliwili*, or **HAWAIIAN CORAL TREE** (*Erythrina sandwicensis*), with its swollen orange trunks and red, orange or cream, pea-like flower-clusters, provides splashes of bright color in spring.

Maui's native **PRICKLY POPPY** (*Argemone glauca*) is adapted to live in arid regions; watch for it along Kaupo Road. Its tissues contain opiates, utilized by ancient Hawaiians for alleviating pains such as toothaches.

Upslope from Kaupo lies **MANAWAINUI VALLEY.** Ribbons of water pour over its upper precipice at 4400 feet in a succession of narrow falls and plunge pools. If the rain is fresh and the afternoon lighting just right, one may be lucky enough to see a half-dozen or more distant falls, framed by a rainbow. This deeply-dissected elliptical depression harbors some of Maui's remnant *koa* forests clinging to its rugged walls, just out of reach of nibbling, pesty feral goats.

FORESTS of *'ohi'a* and *koa,* together with other native hardwoods, formerly stretched half-way around Haleakala. Fire, grazing and goats have depleted the land so that only remnants such as this, adjacent to a moist gully at 5300 feet, remain.

An escaped garden ornamental spread by fruit-eating birds such as mynahs, **LANTANA** *(Lantana camara)* is such a weedy pest that over the last 80 years many insect parasites have been introduced in attempts to control it. Try hiking through it in shorts and you'll realize why farmers detest it. Not only do its prickly branches and pungent leaves deter cattle, but its blackberry-like fruits germinate everywhere, quickly destroying large areas of potentially useful rangeland.

The lush rolling green pastures of **ULUPALAKUA RANCH** introduce us to the civilized world again. In a few more miles you will reach Kula Highway (Rte. 37), a "real road." Located on a corner ridge, Ulupalakua catches more clouds than anywhere else along this entire slope.

Since the mid-70's, several **CAVES AND COLLAPSED LAVA TUBES** on Haleakala's southern slopes have unearthed a remarkable collection of recently extinct bird bones, dating back only a few hundred years. Along with similar sites on other islands, thus far almost *50 previously unknown species of native birds,* somehow trapped in these caverns, have been excavated. Such exciting finds, which teach us much about pre-Western life in Hawaii, include large flightless geese and ibises, crows, eagles, owls and a variety of forest birds. The egg (left) is of a large flightless goose, found near Ulupalakua Ranch. For comparison, a *nene* egg, a fairly large flying goose, is barely bigger than a chicken's egg. The parent of this egg stood three to four feet tall.

Ulupalakua is Maui's noted **WINE-GROWING** area. Tedeschi Vineyards produce champagne, white, rose and pineapple wines. Their tasting room is adjacent to the highway near Ulupakakua Ranch. It is best reached from Route 37, the Kula Highway.

A close view of **JACARANDA:** shapely purple bells.

A picturesque **RURAL COTTAGE IN KULA** beside a glorious, spring blooming jacaranda tree (*Jacaranda mimosaefolia*).

ENVIRONMENTAL ALERT

Maui, situated at 21° N latitude in the oceanic subtropics, is an ideal adopted home for introduced tropical plants. Most thrive in gardens and landscaping, presenting few problems. However, some escape into natural or semi-natural ecosystems and literally "run wild." The 1970s and 1980s experienced a proliferation of now-familiar pests on Maui such as strawberry guava (*Psidium cattleianum*); "inkberry" (*Ardisia elliptica*); yellow, white, and kahili gingers (*Hedychium* spp); Java plum (*Syzygium cuminii*); and African tulip tree (*Spathodea campanulata*).

The 1990s ushered in more menacing species, two so virulent they are capable of *completely and rapidly wiping out Maui's lowland and upland forests.* The most lethal offender is *Miconia calvescens*, called "purple plague" or "green cancer" in Tahiti, where it has aggressively invaded forests from sea level to 4,260 feet in less than 25 years. The other is cane tibouchina (*Tibouchina herbacea*).

Over 60% of the main island of Tahiti is now dominated by "purple plague's" thick, dark groves, which grow to 60 feet tall. Today, one-quarter of Tahiti's native plant species are nearly extinct.

Piles of burning "purple plague" (*Miconia calvescens*), Hana.

"Purple plague" and Koster's curse (*Clidemia hirta*). The latter is already pestiferous on Oahu (250,000 acres of public and private lands) and in forests throughout Hawaii.

Despite enormous expenses of time and money, Maui is poised for a similar scenario. "Purple plague" competes with feral pigs as the most serious threat to conservation in Hawaii. Its potential impact is far greater than all other noxious plants combined. "Purple plague's" continued encroachment into Maui's forests will render all past, present, and future conservation efforts futile, since it crowds out *all established forms of life.* Not even common birds, insects, and plants can survive its onslaught.

"Purple plague's" horticultural name is velvet leaf (*Miconia calvescens*). In its native tropical America, where it colonizes light gaps, its populations are balanced by natural controls (insects, diseases), absent in Hawaii where, under favorable conditions, a three-foot

Most of the greenery visible is "purple plague," crowding out plants and animals unique to Tahiti. Maui is poised for an identical situation.

square experimental plot produced 18,000 seedlings in 6 months! Admittedly attractive, it is esteemed for its large (to two feet long), velvety leaves, shiny green above and bright purple below. Note the **three bold leaf veins,** a characteristic of its family, Melastomataceae.*

WHAT YOU CAN DO: pleas from noxious plant experts

1. Whenever possible, destroy "purple plague" plants. Look for them while driving around. Report sightings to the State Department of Agriculture, Pest and Weed Control Specialists (phone 871-5656) or Haleakala National Park (572-1983). Look particularly along the Hana Highway from Huelo to Kipahulu. Be specific: use stream names (check the concrete bridges) and landmarks (airports, addresses, waterfalls).

Glory-bush (*Tibouchina urvilleana*) is a pest in Kokee, Kauai, and from Volcano to Glenwood, Island of Hawaii. On Maui, it grows primarily in Kula, where the climate is dry. Should it become a popular garden plant in wetter areas, Maui's forests will suffer irreparably.

2. **No matter how pretty it may be, NEVER buy a purple-flowering bush with prominently 3- or 5-veined leaves. To do so is a personal contribution to the guaranteed destruction of Maui's rainforests, native biota, watersheds, and adjacent coral reefs.** Alert nursery personnel and friends. Already 15 species of melastomes grow unchecked in Hawaii, and almost all are listed as noxious weeds by the State of Hawaii. Those on Maui are treated in this book and pictured opposite.

3. Hikers: scrub boots and equipment after hiking anywhere on Maui or on other islands.

* Some melastomes have 5 or 7 bold veins, counting 2 close to the margin. Three, with many ladderlike cross-veins, is more typical.

Cane tibouchina (*Tibouchina herbacea*), a new scourge on West Maui from Waihee to Honokowai. It is extremely important that this rampant, weedy intruder not be further transported by hikers to East Maui.

Medinilla (*Medinilla magnifica*), recently popular in the Hana area and already officially listed as a noxious weed in Hawaii, may well become the next serious pest on Maui.